Amazing Tales of Plant Survival

Lorin Driggs

Consultants

Matthew Fleming
Horticulturalist
Smithsonian Gardens

Cheryl Lane, M.Ed.
Seventh Grade Science Teacher
Chino Valley Unified School District

Michelle Wertman, M.S.Ed.
Literacy Specialist
New York City Public Schools

Publishing Credits

Rachelle Cracchiolo, M.S.Ed., *Publisher*
Emily R. Smith, M.A.Ed., *SVP of Content Development*
Véronique Bos, *VP of Creative*
Dani Neiley, *Editor*
Robin Erickson, *Senior Art Director*

Smithsonian Enterprises

Avery Naughton, *Licensing Coordinator*
Paige Towler, *Editorial Lead*
Jill Corcoran, *Senior Director, Licensed Publishing*
Brigid Ferraro, *Vice President of New Business and Licensing*
Carol LeBlanc, *President*

Image Credits: p. 17 (bottom) Alamy; p. 21 (inset) Alamy;
p. 24 Getty Images; all other images iStock and/or
Shutterstock or in the public domain

Library of Congress Cataloging-in-Publication Data

Names: Driggs, Lorin, author.
Title: Amazing tales of plant survival / Lorin Driggs.
Description: Huntington Beach, CA : Teacher Created Materials, [2024] |
  Includes index. | Audience: Ages 10+ | Summary: ""A bright green plant
  that looks like a big collection of cushions grows in a high, cold
  desert. An unusual plant with only two leaves has survived for almost
  500 years in Africa. Deep in a swamp, a beautiful plant curls a sticky
  leaf around a fly and digests it. All these plants and more manage to
  survive thanks to some remarkable adaptations!""-- Provided by publisher.
Identifiers: LCCN 2024003662 (print) | LCCN 2024003663 (ebook) | ISBN
  9798765968581 (paperback) | ISBN 9798765968666 (ebook)
Subjects: LCSH: Plants--Adaptation--Juvenile literature. | Plant
  physiology--Juvenile literature.
Classification: LCC QK912 .D75 2024 (print) | LCC QK912 (ebook) | DDC
  571.2--dc23/eng/20240305
LC record available at https://lccn.loc.gov/2024003662
LC ebook record available at https://lccn.loc.gov/2024003663

Smithsonian

TCM | Teacher Created Materials

5482 Argosy Avenue
Huntington Beach, CA 92649
www.tcmpub.com
ISBN 979-8-7659-6858-1
© 2025 Teacher Created Materials, Inc.
Printed by: 51497
Printed in : China

Table of Contents

The Importance of Plants

The next time you're outside, take a close look at a tree, a bush, or any plant you see. It may not seem special, but there's a big story there. One way or another, every living being on Earth depends on plants for survival. That includes you! All living things eat plants, or they eat animals that eat plants. Through **photosynthesis**, plants take in the carbon dioxide people and animals breathe out. Then, plants release oxygen that people and animals need to breathe in. Plants also provide many benefits besides food and oxygen, including shelter and protection for animals to raise their young.

Plants can be as different from one another as an ant is from an antelope. Some plants will feed you, some will sting you, some will stab you, and some will make you say, "How beautiful!" Some plants are enormous, and some are so small that they're almost invisible. Plants can be found just about everywhere on land. They're also in oceans, lakes, rivers, and streams. They can be found in the coldest, hottest, sandiest, rockiest, and driest places on Earth!

This pothos plant protects a tree frog from rain.

Plants that survive and thrive in places that seem intolerable are called *extremophiles*. These plants exist in harsh environments around the world. Often, they have special features or behaviors that help them survive. Let's explore some of the plants that live in these places, along with some plants that are extraordinary for other reasons.

hedgehog cactus

Feeding Creativity

Artists throughout time have been and continue to be inspired by plants in all their forms. For example, images of plants can be found in ancient cave art. Sculptors and architects make masterpieces out of wood. Musicians make beautiful music with wooden instruments. Trees and flowers inspire poets and novelists. Plants feed humans' creative spirits!

Plants Have What It Takes

Every part of a plant has a job to do. Even when living conditions are challenging, plant parts must be able to function well. This way, plants can meet their basic survival needs, as well as grow and reproduce.

The Parts That Do the Work

Plant roots serve as both the foundation and the delivery system for nutrients and water. Roots anchor a plant in place and spread out through the soil, giving the plant access to essential water and minerals. The stem supports the plant and carries nutrients and water to its branches and leaves. The leaves are like food factories. They take in energy from the sun and use it to produce the food the entire plant needs to grow.

leaf

flower

fruit

stem

roots

Food for Thought

The energy plants produce is distributed to other living things through the **food chain**. For example, think about a grasshopper eating leaves. The grasshopper gets the energy the plant produced during photosynthesis. The grasshopper slowly begins to grow. Later, a bird spots the grasshopper and snatches it for an evening meal. The plant's energy is now passed up the food chain to the bird. A snake catches the bird the next day. The plant's energy has now been transferred to the snake. A few days later, an owl grabs the snake and eats it. The energy has been transferred to the owl. Eventually, the owl dies. Its body decomposes and enriches the soil. In time, that soil will nurture another plant, another grasshopper will come along, and the cycle will repeat. In that way, plants truly do feed the world!

This grasshopper gets energy from plant leaves.

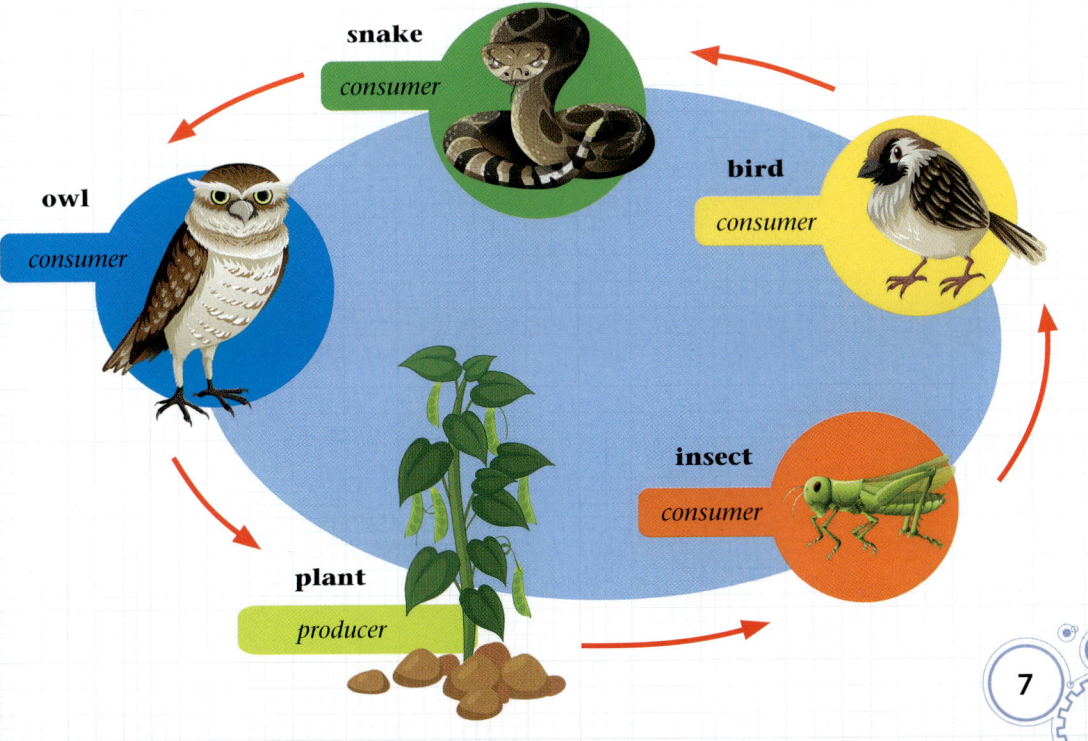

snake
consumer

owl
consumer

bird
consumer

insect
consumer

plant
producer

Making More of the Same

Like all living things, plants reproduce. They do this through sexual or asexual reproduction. This process looks different from plant to plant.

In sexual reproduction, **pollen** needs to be transferred. Pollen is transferred by bees, butterflies, bats, and other **pollinators**. Wind and water can also transfer pollen. This transfer can happen from one flowering plant or **conifer** to another plant of the same kind. The transfer can also be made between

pine cone and seeds

male and female parts of the same plant. Daisies, corn, and oak trees are examples of flowering plants. Pine trees and cypress trees are examples of conifers.

Pollination allows a plant to produce seeds, which is the first stage of the plant life cycle. Seeds come in different packages. Fruits, such as oranges and watermelons, are seed containers. Nuts, bean pods, and pine cones are seed containers, too. Seeds germinate, or begin to grow, in soil or water. Different kinds of seeds germinate at different rates. For some plants, such as sunflowers and beans, it only takes a few days. For other plants, especially trees, it can take months.

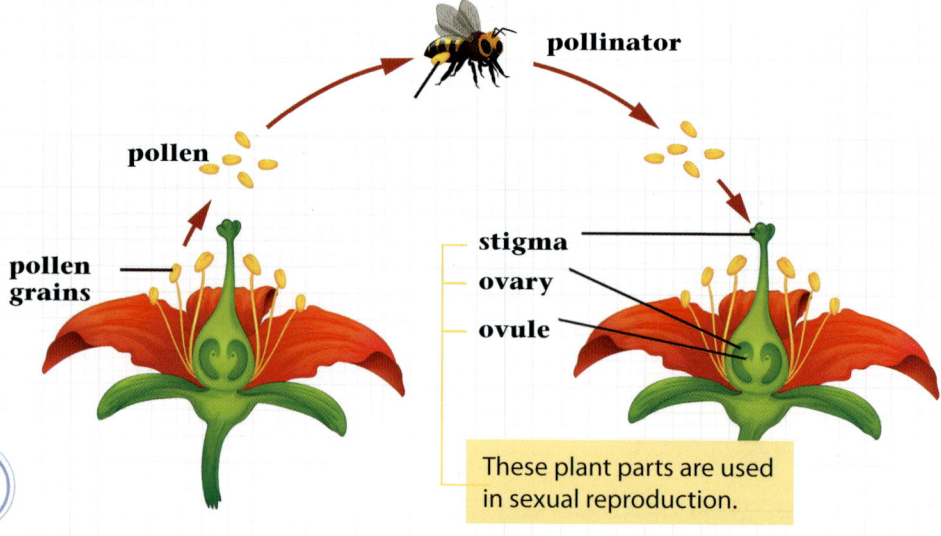

pollinator

pollen

pollen grains

stigma

ovary

ovule

These plant parts are used in sexual reproduction.

On the other hand, asexual reproduction doesn't require pollen. A new plant grows from a part of the parent plant. These parts can include roots, leaves, **tubers**, **bulbs**, **corms**, and **rhizomes**. Potatoes, onions, tulips, and water lilies reproduce this way. Sprouting time varies from plant to plant. For example, potato plants sprout in a couple of weeks. Onions can take several days to two weeks to sprout.

tulip bulbs

FUN FACT

Pollinators have different ways of pollinating plants. For example, bees have small hairs all over their bodies. These hairs trap pollen when they land on flowers. When they land on new flowers, they transfer the pollen from their bodies to the new plants. Bats use their snouts and tongues to get nectar from flowers, and in the process, they get pollen on their faces. When they go to new flowers, the pollen is transferred.

Plants in Very Hot, Dry Places

All living things need water. Plants that grow in places where there is little water face special challenges to their survival.

A Surprising Partnership

A unique partnership exists between two very different organisms—Joshua trees and yucca moths—in the Mojave Desert. This southwestern U.S. desert is covered with tall, spiky-leaved Joshua trees. Although "tree" is in their name, Joshua trees are not trees at all. They are succulents. Succulents have thick parts that can store water. This type of water storage is especially helpful in desert environments.

Across the Mojave, there are two species of Joshua trees and several species of yucca moths. Two of the moth species have a special relationship with Joshua trees. Here's how it works.

Joshua Tree National Park

When spring rains come, Joshua trees produce flowers. The flowers of each species of Joshua tree attract one particular species of yucca moth. This type of moth has a unique structure to its mouth. It is the only insect that can collect and spread the pollen of that particular kind of Joshua tree. The moths' role in the pollination of Joshua trees ensures that those species will survive.

Joshua tree flowers

yucca moth

This relationship benefits the moths, too. They lay their eggs in the flowers of Joshua trees. The caterpillars that emerge from the eggs feed on Joshua tree seeds. This allows the moths to survive as well. The partnership between the plants and the moths allows for survival in a harsh environment.

FUN FACT

Did you know that humans can get involved in plant reproduction? People can choose to propagate plants. Plant propagation is the process of producing a new plant from an existing one. Succulents are one of the easiest types of plants to propagate. For certain types of succulents, all you need is a leaf! Roots, and eventually a new plant, can grow from a leaf. Cuttings taken from stems of succulents can be propagated as well.

The Tree of Life

Plants in the African **savanna** have to survive two extreme seasons: wet and dry. During the wet season, the land experiences large amounts of rainfall. During the rest of the year, there is a severe lack of water. The few trees that grow there have **adaptations** that help them survive the challenging environment. The baobab tree is one example of a plant that adapts well to the savanna.

Baobab trees only have branches at the very tops of their trunks, like a burst of wild hair. Their trunks are huge, and their root systems grow deep and wide. These characteristics are important keys to their survival. In the rainy season, the baobab's roots absorb water and send it up to the trunk and branches, which act like storage tanks. When the dry season comes, the tree survives on that stored water.

Some baobab trees can grow to be nearly 100 feet (30 meters) tall.

The African baobab is often called "the tree of life." It provides shelter for many animals. These include lizards, birds, monkeys, and even elephants. Its flowers are pollinated by small animals, such as bats, that eat the nectar. Its large fruits are consumed by many animals as an important source of water. Humans also use the fruit to make a delicious drink.

SCIENCE

Let's Make a Date

Scientists can find the exact age of trees. They use **dendrochronology** to date tree rings. Growth rings on trees give information about the environment in the past. In the western United States, scientists examined a certain type of pine tree. They found that a bristlecone pine tree growing in the Sierra Nevada Mountains is likely the oldest tree on Earth! It is estimated to be about 5,000 years old.

bristlecone pine

Plants in Very Cold Places

Deserts aren't always hot and covered with shifting sands. Sometimes, they are very cold. They can also be right next to an ocean. Deserts have their own unique plants.

A Green Beauty in a Cold Desert

The Atacama Desert is located on the west coast of South America. It is the driest place on Earth besides the polar regions. The Atacama resembles the surface of Mars. Vast stretches of hard-packed soil are interrupted by rocks, hills, and mountains. But here and there, a burst of bright green appears against the dull landscape. At first glance, it might look like a sprawling, ultra-modern sofa made up of cushions. But this is a plant known as *yareta*. It can be 20 feet (6 meters) across in places.

MATHEMATICS

Slow and Old

Scientists measured how much individual yaretas grew in a year. They estimate that the average growth rate is a little more than half an inch (1.5 centimeters) per year. Based on this, they were able to estimate that some yaretas are more than 3,000 years old.

Conditions in the Atacama are harsh. Plants living there receive almost no rain. Plus, the high altitude exposes them to high winds and high levels of **ultraviolet radiation**. Despite these challenges, some yaretas are more than 3,000 years old. How do they survive?

Answers lie beneath the green surface of each plant. Tangled, woody branches stretch outward in all directions. Trapped dead leaves and stems fall to the ground and decay, adding nutrients to the soil. The tight covering prevents moisture loss and shields against high winds and cold temperatures.

Yareta reproduces the way many other plants do. First, insects pollinate its tiny flowers. Wind spreads the fertilized seeds. When a seed takes root, a new yareta begins its long, slow growth to green beauty.

Yaretas typically grow near or on rocks.

Cotton in the Cold

The Arctic tundra is among the coldest and harshest environments on Earth. It is cold, windy, and dry, and much of it is covered in **permafrost**. Plants that survive there must be adapted for survival in very challenging conditions.

The tundra is treeless because trees require deep root systems that anchor them in the ground. This is not possible where there is permafrost. So, tundra plants tend to grow close to the ground, usually in clusters. Their leaves and stems tend to be small and fuzzy, and their root systems are shallow. These are all adaptations that help these plants conserve heat and grow in the active soil layer above the permafrost.

Short grasses, mosses, and shrubs are some of the plants that grow on the tundra.

Arctic cottongrass, found in much of the Arctic tundra in Alaska and northern Canada, is one of the hardy plants that manages to survive in the tundra. It has skinny, grass-like leaves and stems that can grow to be 28 inches (71 centimeters) tall. Each stem has a seed head at the top that looks like a cotton ball. The cottony fibers protect the seeds inside. The height of the stems and the cottony fibers are key to the plants' ability to reproduce. The wind catches the fibers and carries them away, scattering the seeds. Then, new plants grow where the seeds land and germinate.

arctic cottongrass

FUN FACT

Did you know that more than one million seeds are stored in a mountain deep in the Arctic? In Svalbard, Norway, a global seed vault stores seeds from around the world. Its purpose is to store enough seed backups to prevent massive crop loss in the event of any disasters.

Setting Traps in Soggy Places

Soil quality can have a big effect on plants. Certain places around the world have **acidic** soil. Moderately acidic soil is not usually a problem for plants, but highly acidic soil can be because it is low in nutrients. It is much harder for plants to thrive in this type of soil. It often occurs in very wet places where decaying plant matter builds up over a long period of time. This produces carbon dioxide that reacts with water to create an acid.

This sundew has trapped a fly.

A large group of plants have adapted to this challenge in an unusual way. Since they couldn't gather the nutrients they needed from the soil, they needed to find alternative food sources. You've probably heard of **carnivorous** animals, but how about carnivorous plants? These plants have large appetites for live prey! Some carnivorous plants grow in places such as bogs, swamps, and stream banks.

sundew

Sticky Traps

Sundews grow as far north as Alaska and as far south as southern Africa. They get their name from the sticky droplets of nectar that form on their leaves. These droplets resemble dew when the sun shines on them. These pretty plants don't look dangerous to the mosquitoes and other insects that are attracted to the colorful nectar. But when an insect does land there, it gets stuck. The sundew's leaf then curls up, killing the insect. Digestive juices in the sticky nectar begin to dissolve the insect so the leaves can absorb it.

ENGINEERING

Food Afloat

In the 14th century, the Aztecs braided large amounts of reeds together. They staked them below the water's surface in shallow lake beds. These structures acted like fences that trapped soil. Eventually, the accumulated soil created islands called *chinampas*. The Aztecs began to grow crops on them. Today, similar techniques are used in many parts of the world.

Snap Traps

The Venus flytrap is **native** to bogs in the states of North Carolina and South Carolina. Some people around the world grow these unusual plants in pots or in their gardens. The leaves of these plants look like colorful clamshells with soft, flexible fringe along the edges. But these are the traps! They release a sweet scent that smells like a blend of fruit and flowers. The scent attracts insects. When an insect enters the trap, the clamshell snaps shut. Working like a stomach, the trap releases digestive juices. These juices then break down the prey into a nutritious soup. It can take Venus flytraps anywhere from three to five days to digest their prey.

Venus flytraps can survive for a couple of months without prey.

Suction Traps

Bladderworts use suction to trap their prey. Most species grow in freshwater habitats, either in waterlogged soil or water. Along the stems are little structures known as bladders. When prey swims by and touches a bladder, the bladder acts like a tiny vacuum cleaner. It sucks in water and the prey. This happens in a fraction of a second! Digestive juices dissolve the prey, and the bladder is ready to suction in more food within about 15 minutes. For bladderworts that grow in wet soil, prey consists of very tiny, often microscopic animals. The plants that grow in water trap water fleas, very young fish, mosquito larvae, and even young tadpoles.

bladderwort trap

Bladderwort flowers grow above the traps in the water.

Surprising Superstars

Some plants are remarkable for being able to survive in harsh environments. Some plants are remarkable for their size. Large plants exist all across the world. Here are just a few of these unique species that exist on Earth.

Wonderful, Weird Welwitschia

Most of the Namib Desert is in the African country of Namibia. It is the oldest desert on Earth. Like all deserts, it receives very little rainfall. Some years, no rain falls at all. However, one strip of desert land along the South Atlantic coast is regularly covered in fog. In 1859, that's where a scientist named Friedrich Welwitsch came across an unusual plant. It was named *welwitschia* after his last name.

The average lifespan for welwitschia is 400–1,500 years.

Each plant produces only two leaves that grow to a long length throughout the plant's life. Local people have a word for it that means "two leaves that cannot die." Over time, the two leaves become shredded and tangled until they look like a messy bundle of green ribbon. The largest of these plants are estimated to be 2,000 years old.

Openings on the leaves absorb moisture when fog is present. When the fog is gone, the openings close. This prevents water from evaporating and enables the plants to survive in this very dry place.

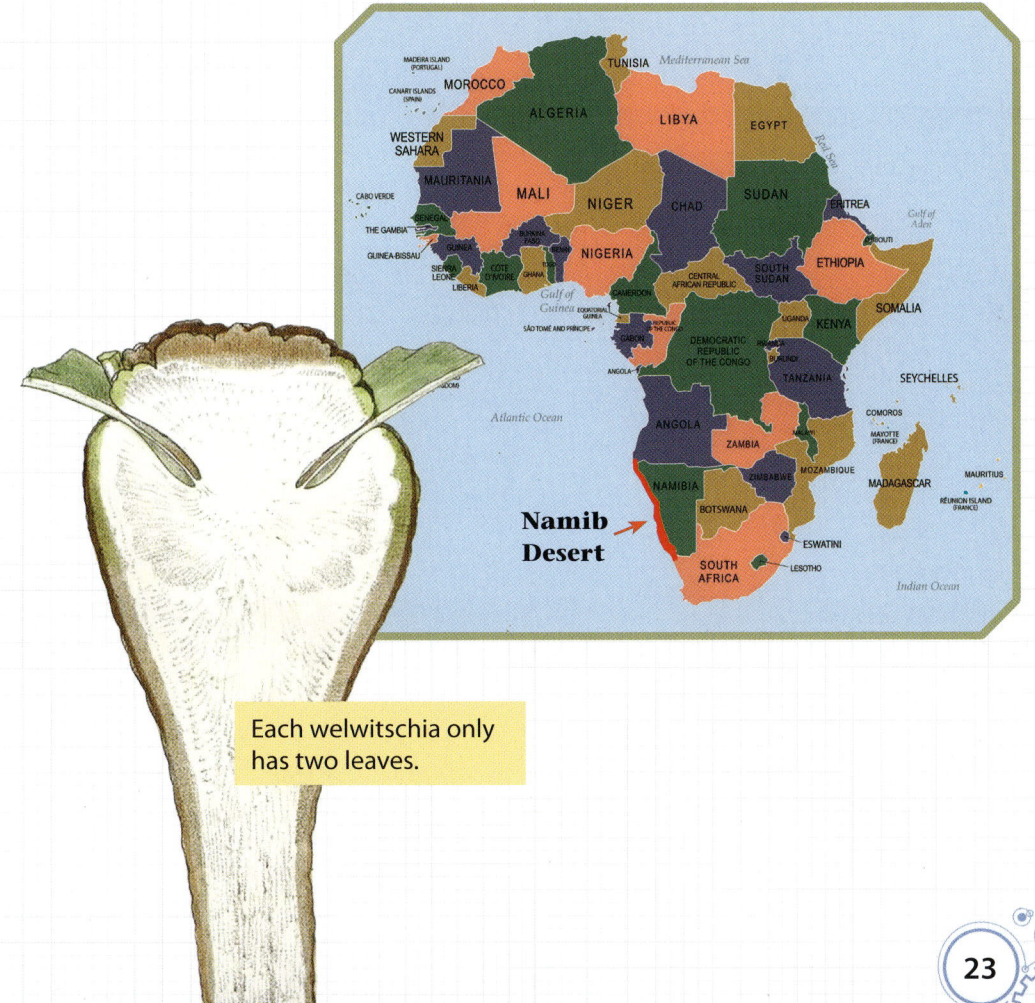

Namib Desert

Each welwitschia only has two leaves.

Captivating Giants

Water lilies have floating circular leaves. In most species, the leaves are 4–8 inches (10–20 centimeters) across. But in the tropical rain forests of Bolivia, Brazil, and Guyana, three species of water lily stand out. They are known as giant water lilies.

Like all water lilies, giant water lilies grow in fresh water. Roots anchor the plants in the mud. They earn the term "giant" because of the size of their leaves and flowers. The leaves of one species can be as wide as 10 feet (3 meters) and can support at least 176 pounds (80 kilograms) of weight.

A botanist carries a giant water lily in a botanical garden.

giant water lilies

Along with their unusual size, giant water lilies have an unusual approach to pollination. First, they produce a flower bud beneath the water's surface. The bud rises upward and breaks the surface. It opens into a flower that is just wide enough to attract and trap a particular species of beetle. The flower's pollen attaches to the beetle. Then, the flower opens just enough to allow the beetle to escape. The beetle then flies to another water lily flower and pollinates it. This pollination process happens over the course of about two days.

water lily flower

TECHNOLOGY

Copying Itself

The largest plant in the world is Poseidon's ribbon weed. This is a type of seagrass that has formed a vast underwater meadow off the coast of Australia. Scientists discovered that it **cloned** itself! They used **DNA** testing to determine that it is all one single organism. During their observations, they also found that the plant is about 4,500 years old.

Why We Dig Plants

Life on Earth operates on a system of energy moving through a food chain. Plants are known as producers because they are the first link in the chain. They produce food for themselves and are a form of energy for consumers. Consumers are the humans and animals who eat the plants.

Humans have learned to safeguard their supplies of food by growing crops. They use science and technology to manage the land and nurture the plants. But in the wild, plants can survive under difficult conditions without human help.

In extreme conditions, plants show diversity and resilience. Plants living in hot, dry places can store water and minimize water loss. Plants in cold places conserve energy and minimize heat loss. The life cycles of many plants are linked to partnerships with pollinators so they can reproduce. In places where the soil lacks nutrients plants need, plants have adapted. They are able to take advantage of alternative food sources—live prey.

Unlike animals, plants can't relocate when conditions change. Their ability to adapt gives them a chance at survival, even in the harshest environments on Earth.

Yaretas thrive in their sandy, dry environment.

Arctic cottongrass begins to sprout again in spring after the winter snow thaws.

A sundew traps a bug.

Baobab trees tower over the landscape.

STEAM CHALLENGE

Define the Problem

As a botanist, you are constantly exploring extreme environments looking for new plant species. You recently discovered an amazing new plant but were unable to remove any samples from the environment. Your camera was also affected by the extreme conditions, so no photographs of the plant exist. However, you need to share information about it with other scientists. Your task is to create a model of your newly discovered plant species to share with others.

Constraints: You may only use the materials provided to you. Your newly discovered plant must live in a real and extreme environment on Earth.

Criteria: Your model plant must show the adaptations that allow it to survive in the extreme environment where it lives. The model plant must show how it protects itself from being eaten and how it protects itself from the weather. The model must also show the unique way it reproduces. You may include any other unique adaptations.

Research and Brainstorm

What are some extreme environments on Earth, and where did you discover this new plant species? What are some adaptations of other plants that help them in extreme environments? What special structures or behaviors could your plant have to help it survive? Which materials will work best for your model?

Design and Build

Sketch two or more designs for your plant model. Label the parts and the materials. Choose the design you think will best meet the criteria. Then, build your plant model.

Test and Improve

Share your model with others. Explain where it was discovered. Explain its special structures and behaviors that help it survive. How can you improve it? Will you set any new goals for your design? What are they? Modify your design and reassess how well it meets the criteria.

Reflect and Share

What about this challenge did you find most interesting? How did you apply your scientific knowledge to complete this challenge? How can models be helpful?

Glossary

acidic—having a lot of acid

adaptations—changes in organisms or their parts that help them survive the conditions of their environments

bulbs—underground part of plants, such as onions and tulips, from which new plants grow

carnivorous—feeding on meat and animal tissues

cloned—made a copy of something that is identical to the original

conifer—any of an order of mostly evergreen trees and shrubs that have leaves resembling needles or scales in shape and include forms (such as pines) with true cones

corms—thick, rounded undergrounds parts of plant stems from which new plants grow

dendrochronology—the science of dating events and variations in an environment in earlier periods of time by studying changes in growth rings in trees

DNA—the information inside the cells of living things that acts like instructions for how to make that organism's body; abbreviation for deoxyribonucleic acid

food chain—an arrangement of plants and animals in which each feeds on the one below it in the chain

native—living or growing naturally in a particular region

permafrost—a permanently frozen layer below the soil surface in very cold regions of Earth

photosynthesis—a chemical process in which plants make their food using water, sunlight, and carbon dioxide

pollen—tiny particles that appear as fine, yellow dust within a flower that can fertilize seeds

pollinators—animals, such as bees, moths, and bats, that transfer pollen between flowers, which later makes seeds grow

rhizomes—thickened, rootlike plant stems that grow horizontally underground and produce new stems and roots

savanna—a mostly flat grassland that contains scattered trees

tubers—short and fleshy underground parts of plant stems from which new plants, such as potatoes, can grow

ultraviolet radiation—rays of energy that come from the sun that are invisible to the human eye

Index

pine trees

CAREER ADVICE
from Smithsonian

Do you want to work with plants?

Here are some tips to keep in mind for the future.

"Get outside more, whether it's planting your own vegetables, visiting a public garden, or walking around your neighborhood. Plants come in all shapes and sizes, so find a few that you enjoy and learn more about their unique characteristics."

– Matthew Fleming, Horticulturalist, Smithsonian Gardens

"Find a tree identification key for your area and teach yourself to the recognize the 10 most common tree species."

– Jake Hendee, Arborist, Smithsonian Gardens